Create and Live
a Life
You Love

Create and Live a Life

a Life

You Love

A guide to the game of life and
how to play it successfully

KERRY EVANS-ALDER

BALBOA
PRESS

A DIVISION OF HAY HOUSE

Balboa Press books may be ordered through booksellers or by contacting:

Balboa Press
A Division of Hay House
1663 Liberty Drive
Bloomington, IN 47403
www.balboapress.com.au
1-(877) 407-4847

ISBN: 978-1-4525-0891-7 (sc)
ISBN: 978-1-4525-0892-4 (e)

The author of this book does not dispense medical advice or prescribe the use
of any technique as a form of treatment for physical, emotional, or medical
problems without the advice of a physician, either directly or indirectly. The
intent of the author is only to offer information of a general nature to help you
in your quest for emotional and spiritual well-being. In the event you use any
of the information in this book for yourself, which is your constitutional right,
the author and the publisher assume no responsibility for your actions.

Printed in the United States of America

Balboa Press rev. date: 02/19/2013

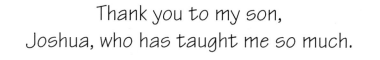

Thank you to my son,
Joshua, who has taught me so much.

CONTENTS

Introduction: Are you happy with your life? ix

Chapter 1: Do You Realise that You Control Your
           Destiny and Can Create a Life You Love? 1

Chapter 2: Your Amazing House...4

Chapter 3: Entering the Room of the Physical Realm 7

Chapter 4: Entering the Room of the Emotional Realm 32

Chapter 5: Entering the Room of the Mental Realm 42

Chapter 6: Entering the Room of the Spiritual Realm 58

Chapter 7: The Keys to the Rooms 90

Chapter 8: Using the Keys 92

Checklist for Creating a Life You Love 95

Special Thanks...99

The Author..101

Recommended Authors 103

INTRODUCTION

Are you happy with your life?

Are you happy with your life?

If you are, that's fantastic. Keep doing what you are already doing. If not, that's okay and quite normal. This book has come into your life at the right time and can help you create a life you love.

From time to time, most people find themselves at a bit of a low spot, financially struggling, feeling restless and very unhappy, wishing life would be different than it is. This is normal because we wouldn't be truly living or growing if there wasn't something else that we wanted to learn, know, have, or do. And we sometimes find ourselves frustrated, stuck and not moving. On that quest, we can find ourselves in deep, dark places, scary places as we enter into the dark night of the soul. We can teeter on the edge of the unknown, entirely unsure of what to do next.

Although I had a happy childhood, I always thought there must have been more to life than the set of cards I had been dealt and that there must have surely been a reason why everyone, including me, was here on Earth. I was right!

These thoughts and inner yearnings have led me on an amazing roller-coaster journey to the other side of the world, with much experience and learning from life itself and some wonderful people I have met along the way. This physical and personal journey has led me to the realisation you can live and have a life you love and that each and every one of us has an important part to play in this game of life.

Enclosed in this book are some of the secrets I have learned, used, and shared with my clients. These secrets give insight into how to create a life you love by entering the four rooms of life, which lead to a life you love.

One thing I have realised is that life is like a house with four rooms. In order to be happy, successful, and abundant in life, you must enter all four rooms daily to access the riches that life has to offer you and to truly create a sustainable life that you love.

Entering these rooms has led me to have and learn that you can create a life you love if you know how and are willing to enter each room on a daily basis.

The amazing Einstein once said, "You cannot solve a problem from the same consciousness that created it. You must see the world anew to make changes." So remember to keep an open mind and remain open to the concepts in this book. Incorporate them on your journey to creating a life you love so that you can see the changes happen in your life.

Amazing things tend to happen when you start this journey, so I recommend you keep a journal to note all of these and to remind yourself that life can be amazing.

Learning is the beginning of wealth.
Learning is the beginning of health.
Learning is the beginning of spirituality.
Searching and learning is where the miracle process all begins.
—Jim Rohn

CHAPTER 1

Do You Realise that You Control Your Destiny and Can Create a Life You Love?

Man is the maker of his own destiny, and I therefore ask you to
become makers of your own destiny.
—Mahatma Gandhi

Are you living the life you want to live? Do you wake up excited every morning, ready to start a fresh, new day in life's grand adventure?

There comes a day in most people's lives when they realise that they are unhappy or things are not as they would like, that perhaps there is more to them and life than just the daily grind they find themselves in.

Although it can sometimes be a painful time, be thankful when that transitional day arrives because it is your *soul* telling and urging you to blossom into the amazing person you are and can become. It's time to become aware and accept the riches that are offered to you in this lifetime.

M. Scott Peck reminds us, "The truth is that our finest moments are most likely to occur when we are feeling deeply uncomfortable, unhappy, or unfulfilled. For it is only in such moments, propelled by our discomfort, that we are likely to step out of our ruts and start searching for different ways or truer answers."

When this day arrives, it marks an important time of choice—a choice to ignore these inner rumblings and keep plodding along as you have been or to hear these inner messages and partake in life's amazing adventure and the abundance the universe has to offer you. It's a time to start seeing the world with a new set of eyes and begin to realise that you are the master of your destiny and that you can have a life you love. It's never too late to start to blossom into the magnificent person you are and live a life you love, for the best place to start is exactly where you are now.

The choice is yours!

If you have decided to blossom into your full potential and gain abundance in your life, then keep reading because today marks the first day of an exciting new future filled with all that your dreams can hold as you learn about your house, its four rooms, and the secrets that lie within them. This information can help you become the master of your destiny and create a life you love.

And the day came when the risk it took to remain tight in the bud was more painful than the risk it took to blossom.

—Anaïs Nin

CHAPTER 2

Your Amazing House

*Everyone **is** a house of four rooms: a physical, a mental,*
an emotional, and a spiritual room.
Most of us tend to live in one room most of the time;
but unless we go into every room every day, even if only to keep it aired,
we are not complete.
—Rummer Godden

Rummer Godden tells us of the old Indian belief that "everyone *is* a house of four rooms: a physical, a mental, an emotional, and a spiritual room. Most of us tend to live in one room most of the time; but unless we go into every room every day, even if only to keep it aired, we are not complete."

To create a life you love and to gain peace, happiness, health, and abundance in your life, people must attend to all these rooms in their own special ways each day. Why? Because the secrets to a rich, happy, healthy, peaceful life lie within entering and using the gifts each room has to offer.

Let's explore how and why this process works.

The house Rummer talks about represents you as a whole person. Your human existence is made up of these four rooms within your house of mind, body, and soul.

The four rooms represent the different aspects of you that make up you as a whole. And for you to be happy and successful in life, you need to be aware that these rooms exist, and you need to learn about the roles they play in you becoming the master of your destiny and creating a life you love.

The four rooms include the following:

- The physical room relates to our physical body and deals with our health and our ability to experience life here on Earth in a grounded way.
- The mental room relates to our thoughts and our ability to co-create an amazing life with the divine.
- The emotional room relates to our emotions and our ability to control them so that we have the ability to be happy, to enjoy life, and to be here on Earth but not of it.
- The spiritual room relates to our divine connection and deals with our ability to connect to our souls (which are our true selves) and our reason for being here on Earth, namely our souls' purpose. Entering this room helps to give us peace and meaning to our lives and what happens in them.

None of these areas can be separated, as they are the whole or the sum total of who you are as a spiritual being having a human journey and make up your human energy system, which is connected to everything and everyone.

These four rooms, which cover the mind, body, and soul, are entwined like the colours of a rainbow, individual in their own right yet not separate, and all have their own special part in affecting your health, wellness, happiness, and abundance in life, not to mention your ability to create a life you love. It takes just as much energy to create a life you love as it does to create a life that is just okay. So let's start creating a life you love by gaining knowledge and access into these four rooms. I recommend you begin a journal or a way of documenting your journey, as magical things begin to happen once you intentionally begin this journey.

CHAPTER 3

Entering the Room of the Physical Realm

Take care of your body. It's the only place you have to live.
—Jim Rohn

The physical room relates to our physical body and deals with our health and our ability to experience life here on Earth in a grounded way. The physical room is about our physical well-being and the impact this has on our lives.

It's important we remember we are spiritual beings, having a human journey. For our spirit to have this amazing earthly experience, it has to have a body as its vehicle. For our soul to thrive, it needs a healthy, grounded physical body to reside in so that it can experience its journey here on Earth. The physical body is the vehicle in which we sense, experience, and live life. Without a well-functioning vehicle, life can become painful, difficult, and lonely.

The physical body is also a fantastic map of how we are travelling in life. In a variety of ways, it tells us if we are on the right road in life, if we are stuck, what is preventing us from moving forward, which areas in our lives are in need of attention, and whether we are on course with our purpose. (This important issue is something we explore more in the spiritual room.)

If we don't learn how to read the physical body like a map, we can eventually experience accidents or pain in the mind or the body. It's the soul and body's way of a signalling we have been travelling off course for some time, and it's time to rethink where we are in life, what we have been doing, and where we are heading. Each part of the body gives us a clue to areas in our lives that need attending, if we have a pain, eczema, swelling, sting, bruising etc. in a particular area it's a sign telling you which area needs attending to—nothing is random or a coincidence in life. Louise Hay has written a great book titled *You Can Heal Your Life*, which gives a comprehensive list of the body, emotions, and diseases, including the following:

- Ailments with your ankles represent being inflexible in life.
- Ailments with your lower back represent financial worries.
- Ailments with your hips represent fears of moving forward on life's journey.
- Ailments with your knees can represent feelings of being stuck. Knees are also about mobility and how we shift with life's changes, tests, and challenges.

The illnesses we have also give clues to emotions or issues that need addressing in our lives:

- Chronic diseases can mean a refusal to change or a fear of a future where you do not feel safe.
- Diabetes can represent a longing for what might have been, a great need to control, and a feeling that the sweetness has gone from life.

Knowing what the body is trying to tell you will give you amazing knowledge and an ability to get your life and health back on track. These messages, when read correctly, allow you to learn what you need to do in order for that to happen. For example, high blood pressure can mean you have a need to look at a long-standing emotional problem that hasn't yet been resolved.

Where do you have ailments in your body, and what signals and messages is your body sending you?

*God whispers to us in our pleasures, speaks to us in our conscience,
but shouts in our pains: it is His megaphone to rouse a deaf world.*

—C. S. Lewis

Gaining access into the physical room

Well-being is attained little by little, yet is no little thing itself.
—Zeno of Citium

The physical body is not something to be idolised at the neglect of our spiritual, mental, and emotional needs, and although it has amazing regeneration abilities, years of abuse and neglect can eventually take their toll.

Good health is a true blessing. Unfortunately, most of us realise how much of a blessing it truly is only when it is taken from us.

Mother Nature has provided our bodies with amazing rejuvenating and healing qualities; all the body needs is the correct ingredients to thrive and allow healing to take place, permitting us to experience wellness and all the joys that it brings.

I encourage you to adopt the topics discussed in the following sections. By doing so, entering and staying in the room of the physical becomes much easier. These are great ways to increase your health and well-being quickly and permanently, opening the door to a healthy body and mind.

The topics recommended are the building blocks of good health. They are simple and well known; however, because of their simplicity, we can become blasé and take them for granted or choose to ignore the need for these health tips for optimal health and wellness.

Remember to drink water.

Our bodies are made up of 60 per cent water, and our brain is composed of 70 per cent water.

Essential to life water is needed for every chemical reaction and function in the body. Our bodies use two litres of water every day to carry out these functions, and that's before we do we do anything strenuous, such as exercise or work.

Without enough water, our bodies cannot function efficiently, so we quickly become tired and depleted. Dehydration can affect our weight, concentration, and mood. A lack of hydration can also cause headaches and bring on fatigue. Not all fluids hydrate the body such as water and herbal teas. Alcohol, tea, coffee, energy drinks and fizzy drinks actually dehydrate the body.

Try to drink two litres of water every day. To help you do this, try the following:

- Keep a bottle of water within easy reach throughout the day. If you don't like drinking water, try adding lemon to it.
- Reduce your intake of soft drinks because they can contain harmful chemicals and leach vital elements from your body, such as calcium.
- Increase your intake of water-filled foods, such as lettuce, cucumbers, avocadoes, and watermelon. As well as the nutritional benefits of eating nutritious foods and adding to your water intake, this action can also help to make you feel full and satisfied.
- Substitute tea and coffee for herbal teas. Try experimenting with different herbs and flavours to see which you prefer because these can be yummy when they are either hot or cold.

Healing Herbal Tea

Herbal teas taste great. They are so easy to make and drink, and they are renowned for their health benefits. Your herbal tea may consist of one main herbal ingredient. It may also be a blend of different herbal ingredients or a blend designed to bring about a specific purpose, such as relaxation, rejuvenation, extra energy, or relief from a specific condition.

To use herbal teas, pour one cup of boiling water over the herbal teabag or chosen herbs. Steep (let herbs remain immersed in hot water) for the designated time normally two-five minutes depending on taste. Remove the teabag or strain off herbs, add honey as a sweetener if desired. Drink the full cup of tea. Such beneficial teas include the following:

- Chamomile is one of the best known and loved herbs for anxiety and relaxation. Traditionally, it has been used as a natural remedy for stress and anxiety.
- Dandelion root can be used to detox and purify the liver and gall bladder of toxins. It is also rich in vitamins A, C, D, and B complex with high levels of minerals.
- Lavender is used to help ease insomnia and calm nervousness and anxiety issues.
- Peppermint makes the perfect after-dinner drink because it aids in digestion and soothes a tummy that is too full.
- Lemon balm is great for calming the nerves and reducing anxiety.
- Chaste berry is a fantastic herb for the treatment of women's issues, such as PMT and/or PMS.

Nutrition

Today, more than 95 per cent of all chronic disease is caused by food choice, toxic food ingredients, nutritional deficiencies and lack of physical exercise.
—Mike Adams

Adequate nutritional intake is extremely important at any time of life, and it is also crucial for gaining good health and maintaining the well-being needed to enter the physical room. Some simple guidelines to remember to help you eat correctly and gain as much nutritional benefit from your meals include many of the steps outlined in this section.

- Eat regular wholesome meals and healthy snacks; this will help keep your blood sugar levels stable. Stable sugar levels help prevent mood swings and strong feelings of hunger, which can often result in overeating.
- Substitute junk food for something yummier like healthy pieces of fresh fruit, nuts, or smoothies. Junk food can zap your energy, whereas pieces of fresh fruit, nuts, natural squeezed juices, and smoothies can increase your energy levels and are an easy way to get your daily intake of vital vitamins and minerals.
- Always try to eat fresh food instead of packaged, refined or processed food.
- Where possible, buy organic quality meat, fruit, and vegetables. Food grown according to organic principles is free from exposure to harmful herbicides and pesticides. Organic agriculture also involves caring for the health of the soil and the ecosystem in which crops and livestock are raised.

Let food be thy medicine and medicine be thy food.
—Hippocrates

Making Life Easy

I realise that sometimes in our busy and hectic schedule, we can neglect our diets, and we may even think that it isn't easy to get our daily nutritional requirements for optimal health.

But it is . . . if you know how!

The answer is green smoothies or juices.

Below, I have added some suggestions. I recommend these because they will help you get your nutritional requirements each day no matter how busy you are. They taste great and are simple, quick, and easy.

Green Smoothies

These are yummy, and it's phenomenal how much nutrition you can actually pack into one glass if you go about it the right way. Green smoothies are generally dairy-free, fruit smoothies with the addition of green, leafy vegetables like spinach, kale, bok choy, lettuce, etc. The beauty of these smoothies is that the fruit disguises the taste of the greens, and it will also disguise the taste of any extra things you want to add in to improve your well-being.

Consider the following recipe for making smoothies:

- 1 banana
- 1-2 of other fruits of your choice (e.g., oranges, apples, kiwi fruit, etc.)
- Pure apple juice or water
- Ice blocks
- 2 big handfuls of greens (e.g., spinach, kale, etc.).
- Some frozen berries
- 1 tablespoon of chia seeds
- 1 tablespoon of LSA

Consider this method as well: It's as simple as putting the banana in the blender with enough apple juice or water to get it whizzing. Once these ingredients are smooth in texture, add your other fruits (after you've cut them up) along with the ice blocks and blend again. You may need to add more apple juice or water if it's not blending well.

When you achieve a smooth consistency, throw everything else in the blender and blend until the texture is nice and creamy. Sprinkle the smoothie with cinnamon as this spice is fantastic in helping regulate blood sugars.

Now drink. Isn't that quick and easy?

You can also individualise your smoothies to suit your own personal requirements. Below are some ideas:

You may want to add some herbs. Coriander helps as a blood purifier and heavy metal detoxifier. Parsley helps to cleanse the kidneys and is an immune system booster. Mint supports the liver.

Add some spirulina powder if you're low in energy.

Need more calcium? Add some sesame seeds.

Need more antioxidants? Add some berries or an avocado.

Need more omega-3 fatty acids in your diet? Then add some chia seeds, hemp oil or an avocado.

If you want protein, add some ground LSA (linseeds, sunflower seeds, and almonds).

Here are a few things to remember:

- The darker the greens, the more packed with nutrition they are. They really are great for us and contain high levels of calcium, folate, iron, fibre, plus lots of vitamins and minerals.
- If you want really creamy smoothies, freeze the banana first or add almond milk instead of water.
- Smoothies are best when people consume them immediately after they make them.
- Don't be scared to try new ingredients and flavours. Things like sprouts, bee pollen, maca powder, dates, and much more all have amazing healing qualities, and these are all great for smoothies.
- Smoothies are excellent for promoting weight loss or maintenance. When our bodies are fuelled and nourished so well, we feel satisfied, and the desire to overeat and eat junk food starts to diminish.
- You can always add your vital greens in the form of powder if you don't want to add fresh greens.
- Or if time or circumstances don't allow for this, then you can add vital greens in the form of powder to apple juice or water and drink this liquid so that you can still gain vital nutritional intake for your day.

Eliminating Toxins

> *By cleansing your body on a regular basis and eliminating as many toxins as possible from your environment, your body can begin to heal itself, prevent disease, and become stronger and more resilient than you ever dreamed possible!*
> —Dr. Edward Group III

The Nemours Foundation describes body toxins in the following way: "A toxin is a chemical or poison that is known to have harmful effects on the body. Toxins can come from food or water, from chemicals used to grow or prepare food, and even from the air that we breathe. Our bodies process those toxins through organs like the liver and kidneys and eliminate them in the form of sweat, urine, and faeces."

The twenty-first century has brought with it an increasing amount of toxins in our everyday living. One of the best and most effective ways you can gain optimal health quickly is by reducing the amount of toxins you ingest and apply to your skin. This takes the strain off your detox organs and helps your body enormously. If the body is continuously trying to detox itself, then those processes don't leave it much energy or time to heal and rejuvenate itself. Hence, many people end up feeling sluggish and fatigued, or they can develop skin problems and illness.

Various toxins you should try to reduce or eliminate include the following:

- Tobacco
- Excess alcohol and fizzy soft drinks
- Excess sugar or artificial sweeteners
- Synthetic substances on the skin. (Our skin is the largest organ in the body, and whatever you apply to it gets absorb, so try to use natural products as much as possible.)

- Processed foods, junk foods, and refined foods
- Pesticides on your fruit and vegetables (If you can't buy organic, then wash all produce.)
- Household chemicals (Try using natural products to clean the home.)

Helping the Body to Detox

Practised for centuries by many cultures around the world, detoxification is about resting, cleaning, and nourishing the body from the inside out. We do this by removing and eliminating toxins and then feeding the body with healthy nutrients. Some of the main organs that the body uses to eliminate and detoxify are the liver, skin, kidneys intestines, lungs, lymphatic system, and bowels. Although the body has its own natural healing and detoxification systems, we can help support these systems when they become overworked or sluggish with simple techniques.

There are many different ways to help support your system and its detoxification, including formal programs and simple changes in diet and lifestyle. Below are some easy and affordable ways to support your body and help these organs in detoxifying your system:

- Our kidneys love and need water to do their work, so try and drink at least eight large glasses of water per day. Drinking water with a dash of lemon juice also assists the liver in the removal of toxins.
- Plant foods, such as vegetables, fruits, whole grains, nuts, seeds, and legumes, will naturally help your body cleanse the digestive system. Plant foods naturally detoxify the body while the fibre helps to get rid of excess cholesterol, fats, and toxins, which tend to build up over time.
- Consider a detox bath. There's no need for pricey spa baths. An effective and inexpensive method to promote detoxification through the skin is with Epsom salts. These hydrated magnesium sulphate salts have many benefits and help promote detoxification. Simply add two to four cups of Epsom salts to your warm bathwater and also enjoy the relaxing effects they produce.
- Drinking herbal teas, such as dandelion root, burdock, and milk thistle, and drinking green tea can help support the kidneys and liver in detoxification.
- Dry skin brushing helps stimulate your lymphatic system, exfoliate your skin, and remove toxins. Special brushes are available at natural health stores.

- Juicing is a great way to add detoxifying and nutrient-rich herbs and fruits into your diet and rest the digestive system.
- Like exercise, saunas are a great way to flush out toxins through the skin by sweating. Remember to drink plenty of water before and after a trip to the sauna and exercising to replace lost fluids.

Get Moving

Those who think they have no time for bodily exercise will sooner or later have to find time for illness.
—Edward Stanley

Movement or exercise is one of the cheapest and easiest ways to improve your health and well-being.

Simple daily movement can build strength, boost energy levels, reduce stress, and cure chronic conditions. Research also suggests that it can slow or even reverse the aging process. By getting out and going for a walk each day or making simple changes like taking the stairs instead of the lift, walking your children to school, or walking to your local store instead of driving, you can make a positive difference in your life.

If exercise has never interested you, don't be afraid to experiment and try different forms of exercise, such as yoga, tai chi and kick-boxing, to see what interests you and what you like. Or you can just start with my favourite, walking. Start with things you like, not what you feel you should do. And make sure you set manageable, attainable goals. Setting goals too high can be frustrating and lead to inactivity because of disappointment.

Look in the local paper or phone book for a recreational centre nearby and see what new and exciting classes have been organized. Perhaps your family or friends would love to get involved as well. Or if you're like me, you may use the opportunity to spend more time with your dog.

Remember to enjoy yourself and have fun.

Are you making time in your week for walking or other forms of exercise?

Fresh Air, Nature, and the Outdoors

Fresh air and nature boosts our well-being and uplifts our spirits. Unfortunately for many people, modern living involves waking up, hopping in the car, working in an air-conditioned office, and driving home through traffic again.

Being in nature is the best way to ground the physical body. When the body is grounded, it can function better and heal itself. Being grounded also affects our ability to feel safe and secure in this world and to trust and know that all of our needs are met, and then we can manifest our desires and become successful. (We will cover this more in the spiritual room.)

When possible, try to spend more time outdoors in nature. This practise may be as simple as eating your lunch in a park instead of your office.

When was the last time you spent some time outdoors in nature?

Relax, Reflect, and Rejuvenate

Learn to get in touch with the silence within yourself and know that everything in this life has a purpose.
—Elisabeth Kubler-Ross

Relax and spend time alone and in silence. Relaxation is essential to your health and well-being. It is known as one of the best antidotes to stress!

Many people avoid spending time alone and in silence. Some are so out of practise that it's almost unnerving to have a quiet moment with themselves because when they do, they can be reminded of what's wrong or uncomfortable in their lives. As a result, they may have stopped trying to carve out that time and filled their lives instead with work, people, or addictions. One of the reasons it can be uncomfortable to sit with ourselves is because when we do, we tend to hear our inner voices, which might question the way we're living or some of the choices we've made. Or these voices may remind us of our inner yearnings or the dreams we have forgotten. Or they can simply remind us it's time to forgive past hurts.

These are the very reasons to spend time alone and in silence, for when we do relax and enjoy this time, our bodies have opportunities to unwind and talk to us. This relaxation time allows you to step out of the hectic world we live in and tune into yourself and listen to the still voice within, which gives you valuable counsel and guidance on the options and paths to take in life.

To begin the process of being with yourself and listening to the wisdom within, you might want to set aside just a few minutes each day to simply sit with yourself. This doesn't mean watching a movie or reading a book, but taking time each day to actually be with yourself in an open way to listen to the wisdom and guidance within.

Are you taking the time to listen to your inner voice?

Nurture Yourself

Looking after yourself and taking time for yourself is essential for your overall physical and emotional health and achieving abundance on all levels.

Many of us have so many responsibilities in life that we forget to take care of ourselves, which can eventually lead to illness and resentment.

While it may seem difficult to prioritise simple pleasures, such as taking a long, warm bath or booking a massage, self-care is an essential part of stress management and letting your soul know you care about yourself.

Florence Scovel Shinn reminds us of the laws of the universes, which tell us that how we treat ourselves will be mirrored by the world around us "as it is within so it is without."

So take the time to show yourself respect, love, and care and watch the world and people around you treat you differently.

Name one nurturing activity you can do for yourself today or sometime during this week.

Read

Books are the quietest and most constant of friends; they are the most accessible and wisest of counsellors, and the most patient of teachers.
—Charles William Eliot

Spend some time each day reading. Reading an inspirational, motivational, or moving quote at the beginning of your day can put you in a better frame of mind so that you can simply enjoy and be grateful for your day. Sometimes reading the life stories of amazing people and learning about the times they overcame obstacles can motivate us to do the same. You may also realise that anything is possible.

From choosing and reading an inspirational quote and receiving its wisdom to learning a new hobby or craft or undertaking more education, these are all avenues in which new and exciting opportunities can present themselves.

The Importance of Sleep

Sleep is your body's natural restorer. Sleep is essential for a person's health and well-being, yet it is surprising how many people don't get enough quality sleep. Much research has been done on sleep, with various studies suggesting that a minimum of eight hours of sleep per night is needed for the body to rest and renew itself.

Some ways to achieve and enjoy a good night's sleep include the following:

- Reduce stimulants two hours before bed (e.g., alcohol, caffeine, fizzy drinks, horror movies, and large meals).
- Read or listen to relaxing music before bed and remove the temptation of watching TV in bed by removing electrical devices.
- Have a soothing drink. Sip a milky drink or a relaxing herbal tea before bed. (Chamomile and lavender has been shown to help calm the body and mind.)
- Relax in a warm bath with added Epsom salts. Take the time to relax your muscles and calm your mind by enjoying a soothing bath just before bed.
- Unwind whilst in bed, listening to a relaxing guided meditation, or visualise your perfect life. Meditation has been shown to create a relaxed mind and body.
- Keep an inviting, clean, comfortable bedroom. Make sure your bedroom is uncluttered, clean, and welcoming. Comfort plays an important part in your sleep pattern. Make sure your mattress is suitable, and the temperature is correct (e.g., cool in the summer and warm in winter).
- Write your worries away. If your mind is full with to-do lists, concerns, and worries when you are going to bed, try writing them down on paper. This way, the mind unwinds, and there's room for peaceful dreams. If you still can't settle and calm the mind before bed, try taking white chestnut flower essence from the Bach flower range, which helps with persistent unwanted thoughts, worry, and constant inner dialogue.

Some Great Daily Habits to Adopt Now to Start Creating a Life You Love

Wake up happy and smile: If you're not happy, keep working on it until you feel better. Before you get out of bed, visualise yourself having a great day. Smile even if you don't feel like it. Studies done by Tara Kraft and Sarah Pressman of the University of Kansas have shown that by making the facial shape of a smile, you will feel better regardless of whether you actually feel happy.

Daily affirmation: Keep a small box of affirmations or a motivational book by the side of your bed because these are a great way to get you inspired for the day. Choose an affirmation or read a positive verse before you get up and take a moment to reflect on the wisdom and inspiration this tool has brought for you today.

Stretch: While you are still in bed, stretch your limbs and *choose* to feel good.

Cleanse: Drink a cup of warm water with a squeeze of lemon when you wake up. Warm lemon water is the perfect morning drink. Lemon kick-starts the metabolism and is a wonderful liver stimulant. It also aids the digestive system and helps promote a healthy immune system.

Move: Indulge in five minutes of stretching, dancing around the house, yoga, tai chi, etc., or if you have time, go for a walk. Movement is a great way to get your blood circulating and release the happy endorphins into the bloodstream.

If mornings are hectic for you, you may wish to do the next part later in the day.

Gratitude Journal: Take the time each day to write in a journal and give thanks for ten things you do have and/or are grateful for (e.g., a working car that gets you safely to work, a beautiful sunny day, etc.)

Meditation: Take ten minutes (at least) each day to do whatever meditation suits you. This may be a visualisation or a process of just being still and listening to music. Journal your thoughts and whatever came to you. (If you are unsure about how to meditate, there is a guide at the back of the book.)

Mindfulness: During the day, bring your thoughts and awareness back to your body. What signals is your body sending you? Ask yourself, "How do I feel? Am I living with integrity? Am I being true to myself?" Acknowledge any patterns of fatigue, numbness, and emotions. Again, you may wish to journal these.

The Key to Entering the Physical Room

The key to entering the physical room is to remember to do everything in life in moderation, no matter what it is. Remember to incorporate the tips previously mentioned in this chapter every day to gain and look after your health. Then you will start to see amazing changes happen. William Londen reminds us "to ensure good health, eat lightly, breathe deeply, live moderately, cultivate cheerfulness, and maintain an interest in life."

Your physical body is the vehicle as well as the map for you to enjoy life's wondrous journey and all its abundance. It is important that you attend to the physical room because it can have an amazing impact on you when you are trying to enter the other three rooms. If you feel unwell, moody, tired, or fatigued, the impetus or ability to enter the other rooms can be greatly compromised.

Unless you put the house of your life—the physical and verbal structures—in order, the urge for exploration of that which is beyond time and space will remain only a wish in the mind. If there is disorder in simple things in life like diet, sleep, exercise, breathing, trying to build a structure of exploration will be like building a house in the sand.
—Vimala Thakar

What will you change today, to make tomorrow better?

CHAPTER 4

Entering the Room of the Emotional Realm

You will begin to heal, when you let go of past hurts, forgive those who
have wronged you and learn to forgive yourself for your mistakes.
—Raw For Beauty

Ah, the room of the emotions! Either people spend too much time in this room and their lives are solely directed by their reactions to everyday events, or they choose not to enter it at all and try to suppress and ignore their emotions by using alcohol, smoking, abusing drugs, or eating and working too much as they feel their emotions are too raw and difficult to deal with.

The emotional room is about understanding our emotions and expressing them appropriately at the correct times. For many, they spend most of their time in the emotional room, hanging on to hurts and wrongdoings, harbouring resentments, and developing bitterness. This then becomes the road map for their lives, being reactive to life rather than proactive. Hence, they become the victims to life and not the creators of lives they love. Now is the time for you to create a life you love. Rather than reacting to the circumstances around you and letting them create and direct your life for you.

Emotions are manifestations of how the body responds to our feelings and attitudes. Our emotions can have a huge effect on our health and how we travel through life, how we view the world, and what we receive from the world around us. The universal laws suggest that our external world is a reflection of our internal world.

If we constantly feel angry or feel like victims, then the universe will give us the very opportunities to manifest these feelings in our lives. So too, if you have feelings of gratitude, then the world will keep giving you more things to be grateful for. Confucius reminds us that "the more man meditates upon good thoughts, the better will be his world and the world at large."

In traditional Chinese medicine, emotions and health are intimately connected. Many Chinese people believe unresolved emotions get stored in the body and contribute to ill health and chronic diseases in the following ways:

- Anger is stored in the liver.
- Resentment is stored in the gall bladder.
- Fear is stored in the kidneys.
- Worry is stored in the spleen.
- A lack of joy is stored in the heart.
- Grief and sadness is stored in the lungs.

Don't ignore your emotions. It is healthy to feel and experience your emotions in the moment; however, you should not continually carry them around like rocks on your back, preventing you from living a life you love. We can help heal ourselves of chronic disease through releasing past memories of trauma, betrayal, heartbreak, and abuse.

It's important to find healthy outlets for your emotions. If you experience grief or sadness, know that it's okay to cry and take some time out to allow yourself time to heal. When you are angry, try to release this feeling through exercising, attending anger management courses, or punching the pillow on your bed instead of another person.

If your emotions are ruling your life, try to become aware of them and acknowledge where they are coming from. Begin to pay attention to the circumstances that might trigger a bad mood or anxious feelings. Various things can trigger our emotions: an unhealthy diet, drinking too much alcohol the night before (the physical room), a negative attitude, feeling as if we don't have any control, conflict (mental room), or a feeling of separateness and being alone (spiritual room). Do what you can to address any known issues that cause your emotions to react by removing obvious stresses from your life and resolving conflicts. Over the following pages, I have given some suggestions that will help you to control your emotions rather than the other way around.

Be Proactive, Not Reactive

Life is 10 per cent what happens to us and 90 per cent how we react to it.
—Dennis P. Kimbro

In the movie *Pirates of the Caribbean*, Captain Jack Sparrow said, "The problem is not the problem. The problem is your attitude about the problem." Life can always seem to have problems, but it is how you react to them that will make the difference on your journey in life and creating a life you love, not the actual problem itself.

When such problems arise, don't react. Instead, try standing back and detaching yourself from the problem. Understand that there is a higher reason for everything, even if you can't see it at that particular moment.

Try looking at problems as the following:

- Ways of revising a situation or path you are taking, as a detour within an adventure.
- God/Universe pointing you in a better direction.
- Opportunities to grow and evolve.
- Opportunity. It's true. There is always a silver lining in any situation. Try looking for it instead of seeing the obvious. (A delayed flight may give you extra special time with a loved one.)
- Opportunities of seeing and understanding someone else's point of view, even if you don't agree.

Remove Judgement

The belief that everyone has a right to their thoughts and actions will free you so that you can live a life you love. It is not our place to judge others. Our responsibility lies within ourselves and the choices we make. Gandhi reminds us to "be the change that you want to see in the world."

Placing the blame or judgment on someone else leaves you powerless to change your experience. Taking responsibility for your beliefs and judgments, gives you the power to change them.
—Byron Katie

Remove Guilt

Many of us wish we could have done things differently or regret past mistakes. It's important to remember that we did what we did at the time with the knowledge and awareness we had then. It's more important to learn and grow from mistakes and move on rather than wallow in past regrets. Consider apologising to the people concerned.

Live and Let Go

It really doesn't matter if the person who hurt you deserves to be forgiven. Forgiveness is a gift you give yourself. It's important to remember not to have any expectations when you forgive someone and that forgiveness does not always lead to healed relationships. Like seasons, relationships have their turn, and if it's time for that relationship to end, it is wise to let those people go along with your anger and wish them well.

The weak can never forgive. Forgiveness is the attribute of the strong.
—Mahatma Gandhi

Live in the Present and Not the Past

When your mind is rambling away with negative emotions and past hurts and you are living in the past, it drowns out the beautiful voice of your soul and the opportunities that await you *now*. Opportunities present themselves in the moment. If we are too busy looking back or worrying about the future, we can miss out on these gifts, which present themselves in the present.

The secret of health for both mind and body is not to mourn for the past, worry about the future, or anticipate troubles, but to live in the present moment wisely and earnestly.
—Buddha

Lifestyle

The lifestyle we live, choices we make, and the food we eat can have a huge impact on our moods and emotions, so remember to eat wholesome meals, drink water, get enough sleep, exercise regularly, and spend time outside in nature and the sunshine. Make a choice to drop the habits that no longer serve you and hinder you from creating a life you love.

The Key to the Emotional Room

Be aware of your emotions and what affects them. Try to be in control of your emotions, not the other way around, where you're constantly reacting and your emotions control and direct you and your life.

To truly begin to do this, let go of past hurts, forgive those who have wronged you, and learn to forgive yourself for your mistakes, for it is only then that you will truly move forward and create a life you love. When we live in the present and realise that we are responsible for our lives, the magic of the universe begins to appear and leads us onto a path towards an amazing life we love.

Don't let your reactive emotions rule your life. Choose to create your life rather than react to circumstances around you?

What will you change today, to make tomorrow better?

CHAPTER 5

Entering the Room of the Mental Realm

Entering the room of the mental realm is about understanding the fact that there are various components to the mind and that you have to use these mental facets wisely in order to create a life you love.

More importantly, it's about realising and understanding that what we think about ourselves and the world around us becomes the truth and our reality, so every thought we think, whether good or bad, is creating our future. Each one of us creates our life experiences by our thoughts and our feelings.

Knowing and integrating this secret into my life was one of the big turning points for me. Realising and knowing this fact of life gives us awareness and freedom, for it is you and only you who creates your life. It's time to stop blaming and giving your power away to other people and circumstances and to start creating a life you love.

Understanding the Mental Realm

The mind is a wonderful tool. If it's used correctly, it can propel us into a life we love, one full of happiness and abundance, or it can keep us trapped in poverty, self-doubt, and fear.

Most people live life back to front, believing that they feel or think in certain ways because of their circumstances, not knowing the truth that it is *their* thoughts and expectations that brought those very circumstances into reality, whether wanted or unwanted.

I realise this can be quite confronting for some people who are not currently in the best circumstances, but you must look on this realisation as empowering and a great thing because now you can begin to create a life you do love with this new awareness.

Now you realise how important it is to be aware of your thoughts as they create your reality. To do this, we must understand that there are various aspects of the mind. For the sake of simplicity in this chapter, I have divided the mind into three sections:

- The functional mind: This is the tool we use to read, learn, calculate, and analyse. The functional mind doesn't talk to us.
- The ego/personality mind: This is the false self, the one talking from the ego or personality. It is normally the babbling voice within a person's head that continually talks throughout the day. It can be the voice of negativity or the one that tells us that we should do this or should do that. This mental chatter gets its information from our conditioning—people who raised us, the culture we grew up in, the media, and other people. The ego voice is often the loudest, and it can tell us that we are no good, we are too fat, we are not pretty, or we are not loved. This voice isn't always the best guide.
- The soul mind: This is our true self and all our possibilities and fullest potential. Initially, the soul voice can speak to us in a quite whisper, but the more we learn to quiet the ego mind, align with our soul's purpose, and spend time in meditation, the louder and clearer the soul voice becomes. It is the voice of wisdom and your best guide.

Using the Mind to Create a Life We Love

The greatest discovery is, that human beings,
by changing the inner attitudes of their minds
can change the outer aspects, of their lives
—William James

Now that we know that *we* create our lives with *our* thoughts and beliefs and we realise the mind has various components, it is so important to quiet the ego or the babbling mind. We attract what we focus on. The more we focus on positive aspects, the more we will attract them into our lives and vice versa. Remember that like attracts like, so if you're feeling happy and abundant, then that's what the universe will dish up for you. Bill Meyer reminds us, "Every thought is a seed. If you plant crab apples, don't count on harvesting golden delicious."

Thought power is one of the keys to creating your reality and a life you love. It is important to realise that everything you perceive in the physical world once had its origin in the invisible, inner world of your thoughts and beliefs.

This concept may be new to some people. If so, spend a few moments sitting with this chapter because it is extremely important that you understand and integrate this principle into your life. To become the master of your destiny, you must be aware of and learn to control your dominant, habitual thoughts. By doing this, you will be able to attract into your life that which you want to have and experience as you come to know the truth that your thoughts really do create your reality.

Using the Mind to Attract Abundance and Create a Life You Love

———————————————————— ⸙ ————————————————————

Our thoughts create our reality—where we put our focus
is the direction we tend to go.
—Peter McWilliams

———————————————————— ⸙ ————————————————————

The mind is a wonderful tool when used correctly and positively. When tamed, it can bring us riches and happiness. When left to wander and worry, it can bring us fear, sadness, and ill health. Training the mind is like minding a mischievous child. You have to constantly keep a check on where it is, what it is focusing on, and what it is doing.

Here are some ideas that can initially help you control the ego mind and create a life you love:

Remove Negativity and Replace with Positivity

A negative attitude is the only true handicap.
—Scott Hamilton

It takes the same amount of energy to be negative as it does to be positive in life. Now that you know your thoughts create your reality, there are no more excuses for thinking negatively. Choose to have a positive attitude and not a negative attitude as it truly does have an impact on your life and creating a life you love. Remember we choose the attitude we want to adopt!

Throughout your day become aware of your thoughts and actions. If you find yourself getting involved with idle gossip or seeing a situation from a negative perspective, click your fingers. This little trick helps break the overthinking and negativity. This physical action momentarily interrupts the thought pattern and gives you time to redirect your thoughts and think afresh. Just like anything new, it may take you a few days to get into the new habit of seeing life differently and thinking and acting more positively, but if you want to create a life you love and a new reality for your life, this is the main way to go about doing that.

Dream Big and Visualise Your Ideal Life

All successful people men and women are big dreamers. They imagine what their future could be, ideal in every respect, and then they work every day toward their distant vision, that goal or purpose.
—Brian Tracy

I love letting my imagination wander, thinking big, and visualising my ideal life. Visualisation is the ability to create mental images in your mind, and it is the primary tool for attracting success and prosperity and creating a life you love. Why is visualisation and imagination so important? Because if you can dream it, you can achieve it. As George Bernard Shaw reminds us, "Imagination is the beginning of creation. You imagine what you desire, you will what you imagine and at last you create what you will." Creative visualisation is used by all successful people and can improve your life and help you achieve the success you desire, regardless of your current financial condition, the state of the economy, your circumstances, or your education. Never let anyone tell you daydreaming and using your imagination is a waste of time, for if our ancestor hadn't used their imaginations and visualised a better world, we would still be living in the Stone Age.

As my vision and goals are always evolving just like my circumstances and I are changing, I use every available opportunity I have throughout my day to stay grateful for what I do actually have and to continually visualise the life I love. I do this in many ways at various times:

- Each day before I get out of bed, I visualise myself having the perfect day.
- In the evening as I'm lying in bed, I visualise the life I love just before I fall asleep.
- If I'm waiting to go into an appointment, I utilise this time wisely and visualise the appointment going well. This practise can be employed before a visit to the dentist, a job interview, etc.

- If people or flights are running late, I use this time wisely not to get angry or irritable but to feel blessed I have an opportunity to dream big.
- Whist you are travelling on public transportation, remember that this is also a great time to let your imagination wander.
- Three times a year, I make myself a dream board (also known as a vision board or manifestation board).

Doing a Dream Board

Each person has an ideal, a hope, a dream which represents the soul.
We must give it the warmth of love, the light of understanding and the
essence of encouragement.
—Colby Dorr Dam

A dream/vision board is a great way for you to clarify and to communicate to yourself and the universe that which you desire and wish to achieve. I love doing my vision board. It helps to keep me focused and reminds me of the goals I wish to achieve and the amazing possibilities available as they start to come true. Vision/dream boards are very personal to you and the life you want, so remember to think big and cut out pictures to add to your board to make it more vibrant and alive. Put it in a prominent place to serve as a daily reminder of your aspirations and what you want your life to resemble. Let your imagination wander and have fun.

When I make a dream board, I get myself a brightly coloured A3 piece of thin card or paper and divide it into sections. These sections include various aspects of my life, such as family, holidays, career, spirituality, relationships, finances, etc. On your board, you can put whatever areas you desire and include any aspects of life that you wish to see change in. Then I write how I would love that area to change for the better. For example, my son's car is old and unreliable, so I write my goal for him to obtain a newer, more reliable vehicle, and I then start to visualise him in this new car. I could even take a picture from a magazine of the car he would like and stick it to my board.

In regards to the work area, I may review my business and add new goals that I wish to achieve over the coming months, or if a holiday is something I desire, I may get some brochures from the travel agent and cut out pictures of the places I wish to visit and place them on my board.

The future you see is the future you get. So think and dream big. Be clear about what you want in life and focus your attention on what you can have instead of what you don't have. For success, you need to focus your mind on the things you desire because your thoughts create your reality and because where your focus is pointed is the direction you tend to go.

Lao Tzu reminds us, "Be careful what you water your dreams with. Water them with worry and fear and you will produce weeds that choke the life from your dream. Water them with optimism and solutions and you will cultivate success. Always be on the lookout for ways to turn a problem into an opportunity for success. Always be on the lookout for ways to nurture your dream."

Remove Fear and Replace It with Faith

We should never let our fears hold us back from pursuing our hopes.
—John F. Kennedy

Fear is probably one of the biggest emotions that holds us back in life and keeps us from attaining the life we love.

Fear can be used as the obstacle to stop you moving forward, a lack of faith and not trusting in yourself or God/Universe to flow and to provide for you, and used as an easier option instead of employing courage.

If fear is holding you back from creating a life you love, try sitting quietly for ten minutes with your feet uncrossed, breathing deeply and slowly (both in and out). When you feel relaxed, think of a dream or a situation you would love to have or change, one where fear is preventing you from achieving this transformation. When you're ready, ask yourself, "What am I really afraid of?" Be true to yourself and stick with the first answer that pops into your mind. You may be surprised at the answer! This exercise can be done continually throughout your life when you feel fear is holding you back and you need some clarity on how to move forward.

When fear does raises it head, Neale Donald Walsch lovingly reminds us, "FEAR is an acronym in the English language for 'False Evidence Appearing Real.'"

The key to success is to focus our conscious mind on things we desire not things we fear.
—Brian Tracy

Action

Commitment leads to action. Action brings your dream closer.
—Marcia Wieder

Now that you know what your dreams and goals are and have removed any fear of achieving them, it's time to take some action towards these goals/dreams.

We now know our thoughts help create our realities and tools like the vision/dream board help us communicate with ourselves and the universe in regards to what we would love in our lives.

Once this is done, the universe will start to bring opportunities our way to help us achieve all that we desire. But action is still required on your part.

For example, if you wish to gain employment, the universe may bring you the opportunity of sitting next to someone who tells you about the job or someone may give you a newspaper with a job advert in it. Hence, the universe has done its part, but now you have to do your part and take action and call for an interview and present yourself accordingly.

Here's another example: You are a currently a cleaner and your dream is to become a doctor, you may not be able to afford to go to medical school, or you may not have the relevant qualifications at this time. So the universe may play its part by giving you a pay rise so that you can attend evening college to get the grades you need to enter university. But again, you have to do your part and enrol and turn up for classes.

The universe works in mysterious ways and always knows best. When you ask for something, the universe will deliver, but perhaps not always in the way you expected. We can't always see the bigger picture, and as the Dalai Lama reminds us, "Remember that not getting what you want is sometimes a wonderful stroke of luck." So be open to opportunities that do come your way and always take action because this is another way of giving thanks to the universe for providing.

Taking Action

I have learned that if one advances confidently in the direction of his dreams, and endeavours to live the life he has imagined, he will meet with a success unexpected in common hours.
—Henry David Thoreau

A great way to start taking action and see what action is needed to achieve these goals is draw three columns on a sheet of paper. In the first column, write the heading "Where am I now?" Then fill in your personal answer. In the third column, write the heading "Where do I want to be?" or write your goal or dream here. In the middle second column, write the heading "How to get there" or "Action I can take now." Then fill this last column in with the actions you can take immediately to start the process of achieving your goals.

This exercise can be done for anything you want to achieve in life and for creating a life you love.

The Key to the Mental Room

You must realise that your inner thoughts create your outer world. In others words, remember that your thoughts create your reality. Make sure these thoughts are focused on what you want instead of what you don't want. The more we align our thoughts, actions, and words with what we desire, the clearer we are in expressing our truth in the world and the more powerful we are in bringing those desires into reality.

Constantly be aware of your thoughts. If you find yourself dwelling on negative ideas, chose to change them to more positive ones, as Florence Scovel Shinn reminds us the universal law states, "Like attracts like."

Learn to quiet the ego voice and to listen more for the soul voice, which is your true self and the best guide in life.

Whatever the conscious mind thinks and believes,
the subconscious identically creates.
—Brian Adams

What will you change today, to make tomorrow better?

CHAPTER 6

Entering the Room of the Spiritual Realm

The key to this room is often the one least used, least understood, and the most elusive.

One of the reasons for this lack of presence is that everything we deal with in the spiritual room lies within the invisible realm and can't initially be seen by the naked eye. Consequently, there is a need for faith if people desire to enter the spiritual room—faith that there is a loving force greater than us and that the mind can't yet comprehend what the heart knows all too well.

Entering the spiritual room is not about religion, ceremonies, churches, or temples, although these can be pathways on a spiritual journey. It is about understanding that you are a spiritual being that is having a human experience, not the other way around. By understanding this concept, we can start to explore our energy body and align with the incredible guidance and help that lies within us and the invisible realms.

Entering the spiritual room is about realising and remembering the following:

- There is a loving and guiding force greater than you, but this force also is you and connects to you and everything.
- You are an amazing soul with a unique purpose.
- We have spiritual bodies just as we have physical bodies.

Entering the spiritual room is about connecting to and getting to truly know you as a spiritual being as well as learning to follow your inner wisdom and intuition.

Help is there if you only ask!

When entering the spiritual room, you begin to realise that there is a force bigger than yourself, one that is ever-present and ever-loving, just waiting for the opportunity to enter and become a bigger part of your life. All you have to do is ask, and it is there. Some of the guises this force presents itself in are angels and guides that work in the invisible realm, yet the results of their work can be clearly seen in our physical world. Remember, these loving guides and angels are always on standby, ready to help and guide, but to do this, they need permission from us to step in and help. So remember to continually ask for help and guidance and remember to give thanks when they do indeed help you.

It's this loving force, which goes by many names, that can give us guidance, comfort, love, peace, and so much more, especially in times of need. As we all know, life is challenging and changing at a rapid pace with much chaos and turbulence. The ability and awareness to enter this room will give you much strength, understanding, and comfort in these trying times.

"One night I dreamed I was walking along the beach with the Lord. Many scenes from my life flashed across the sky.

In each scene I noticed footprints in the sand. Sometimes there were two sets of footprints, other times there was one only.

This bothered me because I noticed that during the low periods of my life, when I was suffering from anguish, sorrow or defeat, I could see only one set of footprints, so I said to the Lord,

"You promised me Lord, that if I followed you, you would walk with me always. But I have noticed that during the most trying periods of my life there has only been one set of footprints in the sand. Why, when I needed you most, have you not been there for me?"

The Lord replied, "The years when you have seen only one set of footprints, my child, is when I carried you."

Mary Stevenson

Remembering Who We Really Are

We ask ourselves,
"Who am I to be brilliant, gorgeous, talented, fabulous?"
Actually who are you not to be?
—Marianne Williamson

Have you ever wondered why you are here on planet Earth or why certain people are in your life? Have you ever asked, "For what reason was I born?"

Many people do not realise that they are souls having human experiences and that they are unique, amazing individuals with unique purposes in this life. This is called your soul purpose. Each of us has arrived here with a very specific plan for what we can accomplish and experience in a given lifetime, and we have been given the talents and gifts to fulfil our purposes as well. Woodrow Wilson reminds us beautifully, "You are not here merely to make a living. You are here, In order to enable the world to live more amply, with greater vision and with a finer spirit of hope and achievement. You are here to enrich the world."

Unfortunately, so many people forget this. It is so important to remember that you are a unique individual created in a beautiful way, with your own unique gifts, talents, and reason for being here. Hence, there is no one else like you in this world. As Jean Houston reminds us, "We all have the extraordinary coded inside of us, waiting to be released." So start to realise and believe this. Take your place and start to enjoy the many beautiful wonders the universe has in store for you.

Understanding your soul purpose

*The purpose of life is to discover your gift. The meaning
of life is giving your gift away.*
—David Viscott

Your soul purpose is a unique agreement that you made with the universe before you were born. Yes, that's correct. You read correctly. It started before you were born. We all choose our family, destiny points, and our soul's purpose before we enter the Earth plane. The rest we fill in along the way with our free will and choices. Your soul purpose is a unique purpose to serve humanity and yourself in a particular way this lifetime.

Unfortunately, when we are born, we forget this unique purpose. It is only through life's lessons on this earth journey that we start to remember what our talents and unique purposes here on the planet Earth are.

Discovering our purpose can be challenging because sometimes we become so disconnected from our intrinsic gifts and who we truly are. This is quite normal and occurs for all of us as we develop our personalities or false selves and the skills needed to conform to the mould sometimes created for us by family, friends, culture, and environment. The art to following and living your soul's purpose is to be true to you and you alone. Steve Jobs, the founder of Apple, once said, "Your time is limited, so don't waste it living someone else's life. Don't be trapped by dogma—which is living with the results of other people's thinking. Don't let the noise of others' opinions drown out your own inner voice. And most importantly, have the courage to follow your heart and intuition. They somehow already know what you truly want to become. Everything else is secondary."

We become so busy being who we think we're supposed to be that we forget who we truly are and ignore that inner voice that keeps trying to remind us. Many forget that they are amazing individuals with gifts, talents, and unique purposes. These treasures are just waiting to be found within. Yet it is surprising how many never open their packages.

Often people attempt to live their lives backwards:
they try to have more things, or more money,
in order to do more of what they want so they will be happier.
The way it actually works is the reverse.
You must first be who you really are, then, do what you need to do,
in order to have what you want.
—Margaret Young

Remembering Who You Truly Are

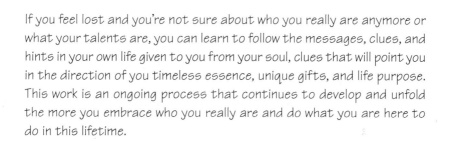

Success means having the courage, the determination, and the will to become the person you believe you were meant to be.
—George Sheehan

If you feel lost and you're not sure about who you really are anymore or what your talents are, you can learn to follow the messages, clues, and hints in your own life given to you from your soul, clues that will point you in the direction of you timeless essence, unique gifts, and life purpose. This work is an ongoing process that continues to develop and unfold the more you embrace who you really are and do what you are here to do in this lifetime.

For some ideas for remembering who you truly are and finding your gifts and talents, ask yourself the following questions:

- What am I doing when the time seems to go very quickly?
- What do I love doing?
- What are my current gifts and talents?
- What would I do if time, money, and responsibilities weren't issues?
- As a child, what did I love to do or want to be?
- What hobbies do I love or would like to start?

In meditation, actually ask your soul what your purpose is during this lifetime and take the time to listen. Write the answers down on paper or in your journal because you will begin to see a common thread between them all. Then these answers will start to give you an idea about what your soul loves, who you truly are, and what you have come here to share.

Your soul purpose will be unique to you. Not all of us have come here to be in the spotlight and have an enormous impact on many people like Oprah Winfrey or the Dalai Lama. For some of us, it may be to be the best parents we can be to our children or even to be a great farmer so that others can eat; however, each person is just as important as the other in the game of life, and each has their own unique part to play.

Remember your soul purpose is not something you can just find. You're living your purpose now to some degree, but the more you can align yourself with who you truly are and not your ego personality, the clearer your purpose becomes and the more fully you live it. Lauren Gorgo explains this beautifully:

> So then, it can be said that our life-purpose is in this now moment, not based in some future concept or alternate universe. It is the small things that we incorporate into our lives, the big things that we eliminate because they no longer serve us, and the courage to let go of an outworn life that no longer matches our current perceptions. This is how we make room for our passions and create the space to allow our missions of joy to unfold before us . . . but only as we are prepared to receive them. We must clear our canvases of mis-creation to allow our souls to paint the new and higher versions of ourselves and our lives . . . and this is where true joy resides, in the creation, expression and experience of those creations.
>
> To do this, we spend many years in preparation for the actualization of our signature essence, aka soul purpose. It is a process of clearing our emotions and detoxifying our minds and bodies for purification to allow the light of our souls to become clearer. We must heal ourselves of chronic disease through releasing past memories of betrayal, heartbreak and abuse; we must let go of our co-dependent behaviours and addictions; heal our relationships and find forgiveness in ourselves and in our perpetrators. As each of us engage in our personal metamorphosis, however it unfolds, we often find ourselves alone, rejected by and isolated from our peers, families and even our own mates. But ultimately in all of this, we learn to stand in our power

and take responsibility for our lives and happiness by exploring the whole gamut of human suffering . . . that is, until the polarity of extremes is no longer necessary for our growth.

And this by far, has global ramifications. When we engage in this self-exploration we heal ourselves and provide the example for others so that one by one, gender by gender, race by race, culture by culture, community by community, and nation by nation, we can eventually heal the world . . . or at the very least, set it in motion. Our gifts are in these challenges and years of stretching and growing into our new skins. Our opportunities then, reside in this suffering and often our "life purpose" is hidden behind those challenges and reveals itself in sharing our path and what we learned upon it with others in a way that will encourage each of them to take the required steps to total freedom.

Ultimately then, we all have the same life-purpose . . . to heal ourselves by finding our joy and then sharing that joy to inspire others.

Getting in Touch with Your True Self

Face new challenges, seize new opportunities,
test your resources against the unknown,
And in the process, discover your own unique potential.
—John Amatt

To get in touch with your true self, namely your soul, you must act on your intuition or gut feelings as this is the language of the soul. Spend time alone and in silence. This allows you to connect to your heart and hear and learn from the guidance within yourself. Do whatever your heart leads you to do because it is through the heart that your soul speaks to you. Nurture your soul regularly by doing what you love. This might be as simple as buying yourself flowers or spending time in nature.

Ways to Help You Enter the Spiritual Room

Prayer: Realise that you are not alone and that there is a higher guidance to help you on your journey. All you have to do is ask for this help.

You are never alone or helpless.
The force that guides the stars guides you too.
—Shri Shri

Detachment: Learn the art of detachment. Worrying is of no help to anyone. Instead, simply ask God (or whatever name you use to recognise the force greater than you and the creator of all) to place a protective white light around the people you love and their situations, for this has more helping power than worry does. Learn to detach from the worries of the world and have faith that the universe is taking care of everything. This does not mean you must become numb to what is happening around you, but realising and taking the belief from the scripters of "thy will not mine," which is having the faith that God/Universe knows best, for it has a far better view and greater understanding than we do. By practising the art of detachment, you learn to be in the world but not of it—meaning you can participate in the game of life but under your rules.

Faith is believing that God is going to take you places
before you even get there.
—Matthew Barnett

Surrender: When things don't go according to plan, learn to surrender. Go with the flow and accept all will work out for the best. I know sometimes this can be very difficult, especially if there are loved ones involved. Below is the "Serenity Prayer" by Reinhold Niebuhr, I say to myself in the times when I can't see the bigger picture:

> God, grant me the serenity
> to accept the things I cannot change,
> the courage to change the things I can,
> and the wisdom to know the difference.

Kindness and compassion: Act and filter everything through the heart, not the mind. When the Dalai Lama was asked what his religion was, he simply answered, "Kindness." He reminds us that if you can, help others; if you cannot do that, at least do not harm them. If you want others to be happy, practice compassion. If you want to be happy, practice compassion.

Too often we underestimate the power of a touch, a smile, a kind word, a listening ear, an honest compliment, or the smallest act of caring, all of which have the potential to turn a life around.
—Leo Buscaglia

Prayer and meditation: Spend time in prayer and meditation each day. I can't emphasise this activity enough. Prayer is when you speak to God; meditation is when God speaks to you. It is so important to spend time in prayer and meditation, and it's also crucial to do this in a way that that works for you. Some find it easier to connect and talk to God when they are in nature. Others find it more comforting to kneel at their bed at night, hands clasped. The same goes for meditation. Some people love guided meditations, and others love meditating while they listen to music or gaze at candles. Just do it and do what works for you because the benefits are amazing.

They say it is through prayer that you speak to God
And through meditation God speaks to you.
—Unknown

Joy: Do what you love and what brings you joy. This is not a selfish act but a necessary one. When you are doing what you truly love, you are connecting more with your soul, your reason for being here and sharing your gifts.

Success is not the key to happiness. Happiness is the key to success.
If you love what you are doing, you will be successful.
—Albert Schweitzer

Gratitude journal: Giving thanks and appreciation for what you do have is one of the most powerful ways to increase your well-being and create a life you love. Each day, open your journal and write at least five to ten things you are grateful for in your life. No matter how bad your life currently seems, there is always something to be grateful for. You may have food in your belly. The sun is shining. You have a job. The universe loves a grateful heart and rewards it tenfold.

You simply will not be the same person two months from now after consciously giving thanks each day for the abundance that exists in your life. And you will have set in motion an ancient spiritual law: the more you have and are grateful for, the more will be given you.
—Sarah Ban Breathnach

Our Spiritual Body

The same energy of our Divine Source flows through us, radiates out from us, and illuminates our lives. Understanding and experiencing ourselves as this energy is so empowering! We are made of the same creative energy from which new worlds are born!
—Karen Whitaker

We know we have physical bodies made up liquids, organs, and systems. We also have spiritual bodies that are made up of an energy system consisting of chi, meridians, chakras, and auras.

For many of the ancient civilisations, such as Hindus, Egyptians, Chinese, Greeks, and aboriginals, the chakras were an integrated part of their daily lives. As these ancient civilizations were conquered, vast libraries of knowledge were destroyed. Only a few remnants of information on the chakra system have survived either through the preservation of ancient texts by sacred priesthoods or the oral passage from generation to generation in the traditions of many aboriginal peoples. But thanks to people like Barbara Ann Brennan, Donna Eden, Carolyn Myss, Anodea Judith, Ambika Wauters, Cyndi Dale, and many others, we have once again been educated in the chakra system and the important role it plays in our overall well-being and life.

Our chi is our spiritual life force and flows through our meridians, which flow into our chakras. And we are also encased in an aura. Think of this spiritual mechanism is the same way as the body. We have blood that flows through our veins into organs, and we are also encased in our skin.

When our life force energy becomes disturbed, stagnant, imbalanced, or depleted within our energy field through trauma and negative emotions, disease and illness can begin to take root.

Our spiritual bodies are just as important as our physical bodies, and they have huge impacts on our physical bodies and our abilities to create lives we love. There are seven main energy centres in the body known as chakras. Each chakra is related to different emotions, different parts of the body, and how we view and cope with life in general. Chakras are energy wheels that connect not only with the physical but with the emotional and spiritual aspects of our lives as well. Our chakras balance and distribute life force energy to create homeostasis among all systems and functions within the body. If the energy in any chakra becomes stagnant, then this will have an effect on the corresponding organs, emotions, and life aspects.

Just as the physical body can be a map to indicate where we are stuck in life and what needs attending to so that we can move forward, the chakra system does the same in a spiritual way. Below is an introduction to the chakra system and the seven chakras. The list will begin to give you some insight into your energy /spiritual body. It shows the correlation of each chakra, its corresponding physical organs, the emotions that are affected by each chakra, and how blockages can manifest themselves in our lives. The description also gives you some ideas on how to balance a chakra if you feel it has become unbalanced.

I recommend you spend time studying, understanding, and knowing the chakra system as it gives you the knowledge to allow you to venture and delve further into the four rooms, giving more meaning and the realisation of the continual importance of these four rooms further along on your journey to creating a life you love.

The first chakra is known as the root chakra and is located at the base of the spine.

The colour associated with the root chakra is red.

The root chakra is associated with our basic needs for survival, security, strength, safety, and trust, connecting us with our family and our profession. The root chakra is powerfully related to our contact with the Earth and our ability to be grounded into the earth plane, which is essential to creating a life you love.

The physical body that is connected to this chakra include our bones, knees, legs, hips, ankles, feet, and the adrenal glands. If there is an imbalance in this chakra, we may experience obesity, anorexia nervosa, knee or ankle problems, etc.

If this chakra is disrupted, it can affect our ability to cope, adapt to change, be successful, and maintain healthy relationships with money, food, etc.

If this chakra is imbalanced, now is the time to spend more time in and connecting to nature and to reduce or eliminate activities that cause us to feel ungrounded (e.g., drug abuse and addictions). Colour has an amazing impact on balancing the chakras. To help balance this chakra, wear the colour red or/and eat red foods, such as strawberries, to help you become more grounded.

Affirmation

"I am safe and all my needs are met"

A Visualisation Meditation to Help Balance the Root Chakra

Relax and gently close your eyes.
Breathe deeply in and out. Then visualise yourself climbing onto the
back of an elephant.
Allow the elephant to take you on a beautiful journey.
He is taking you into a cave where you feel safe and secure.
As you go deeper and deeper into the cave,
You notice there are different pathways outwards.
Allow the elephant to lead you onto a path.
Where do you go?
What do you see?
Begin a journal and write all that you see or hear.

The second chakra is known as the sacral chakra and is located beneath the navel.

The colour associated with this chakra is orange.

The sacral chakra affects the areas of abundance, sensuality, sexuality, creativity, success, joy, relationships, and desires.

The areas of the physical body that are connected to this chakra include sexual organs, reproductive system, bladder, kidneys, and the large intestine. Imbalances in the sacral chakra can cause kidney weakness, constipation, and fertility issues.

If our sacral chakra is disrupted, it can affect our ability to be creative, to have successful relationships with others, and to be happy.

If this chakra is imbalanced, then now is the time to awaken your true inner desires and know that you have the ability to create a life you love, to become aware that your thoughts create your reality so that you can have fun and use your imagination, and to realise your true desires as well as the fact that you are the master of your journey so that you can create the life you want. This journey starts with you visualising what you want and then planting seeds so this new chapter in your life can begin to germinate/sprout. It's time to awaken your inner goddess, create healthy boundaries, have fun, and use your imagination to realise your true desires. Colour has an amazing impact on balancing the chakras. To help balance this chakra, wear the colour orange or/and eat orange foods like pumpkins.

Affirmation

"I now create the life I want."

A Visualisation Meditation to Help Balance the sacral Chakra

Relax and gently close your eyes.
Breathe deeply in and out and then visualise yourself at night in a
boat on a beautiful calm sea.
There is a large silvery full moon above you,
its light shimmering on the water.
Dolphins begin to swim and play around the boat, so you decide to
dive into the shimmering, calm water
and follow them.
Where do they go?
Allow yourself to go on this journey.
Then return to the boat.
Begin a journal and write all that you see and hear.

The third chakra in known as the solar plexus chakra and is located in the abdomen area.

The solar plexus chakra affects the areas of confidence, self-esteem, empowerment, ambition, action, courage, and joy for life.

The associated colour is yellow.

The solar plexus chakra is known as the seat of our emotions. Blockages in this chakra can manifest as anger, sense of victimization, self-pity, and resentment. The solar plexus centre deals with our sense of self.

The areas of the physical body that are connected to this chakra include the stomach, liver, gall bladder, pancreas, and small intestine. Imbalances in the solar plexus chakra can cause digestive difficulties, liver problems, diabetes, etc.

If our solar plexus chakra is disrupted, it can affect our ability to successful in life.

If this chakra is imbalanced, then now is the time to remember that you are an amazing individual with amazing gifts and abilities and that you have the confidence and courage to follow your ambitions. Employ courage to start making decisions and realise you are always on the right path. Take the action needed to be successful and happy in your life. Colour has an amazing impact on balancing the chakras. To help balance this chakra, wear the colour yellow or/and eat yellow foods like bananas.

Affirmation

"I now take actions towards my goals."

A Visualisation Meditation to Help Balance the Solar Plexus Chakra

Relax and gently close your eyes.
Breathe deeply in and out and then visualise yourself
sitting in front of a glowing fire, holding a crystal ball.
Watch the reflection of the flames in the ball.
See if images of situations that have damaged
your sense of self or your confidence emerge.
Then ask that the negative images be transformed by the fire
and replaced by beautiful new images of the real you.
Begin a journal and write down the positive new image you see of
yourself.

The fourth chakra is known as the heart chakra and is located in a similar position to our physical heart.

The associated colour is green.

The heart chakra is our emotional centre, responding to our feelings of love and joy. This chakra affects our abilities for compassion, love of self and others, acceptance, romance, and gratitude.

The areas of the physical body that are connected to this chakra include the heart, lungs, circulatory system, shoulders, and upper back. Imbalances in the heart chakra can manifest as heart, respiratory, or immune system problems.

If your heart chakra is disrupted, it can affect your ability to be compassionate and to give and receive love.

If this chakra is imbalanced, then now is the time to release grief, to love and accept yourself as you are today, to choose the path of forgiveness and have compassion for others, to start making choices based on the heart instead of the head, to stop judging others and allow others to be who they want to be, and finally, to allow romance into your life. Colour has an amazing impact on balancing the chakras. To help balance this chakra, wear the colours pink or green or/and eat pink or green coloured foods like watermelons and avocados.

Affirmation

"I recognise the beauty in me and all that surrounds me."

A Visualisation Meditation to Help Balance the Heart Chakra

Relax and gently close your eyes.
Breathe deeply in and out and then visualise
a big pink rosebud in the centre of your heart.
As you breathe in and out, slowly the bud
begins to open one petal at a time.
Once the rose is fully open and blossomed,
you begin to see people in the centre of the rose.
Some of these people are familiar to you.
There are people present to whom you need to talk.
So you find them and make your peace
and forgive them in whatever way you need to.

You may be surprised—who pops up!

The fifth chakra is known as the throat chakra and is located parallel to the thyroid gland.

The colour associated with this chakra is sky blue.

The throat chakra is associated with communication, the soul's purpose, truth, wisdom, and choice.

The areas of the physical body that are connected to this chakra include the throat, neck, thyroid, mouth, jaw, teeth, tongue, and ears. Imbalances in this chakra can manifest themselves as sore throats, tonsillitis, thyroid problems, stiff necks, and toothaches.

If this chakra is imbalanced, you may want to try enacting the following:

- Release any preconceived ideas you had about you and how your life should be.
- Learn to listen and follow your soul's purpose.
- Accept who you truly are and be true to yourself.
- Listen to your inner voice, your soul's true GPS system in life.
- Become greater than you ever imagined.
- Realise that life is a journey and accept that we are here to learn and that everything happens for a reason.
- Have self-expression and communicate your needs and requirements.
- Hold no expectations and give up the need to know why things happen as they do.
- Trust that the unscheduled events in our lives are a form of spiritual direction.
- Colour has an amazing impact on balancing the chakras. Try wearing the colours blue or turquoise, especially as a scarf or tie around the neck.

Affirmation

"I am now true to me."

A Visualisation Meditation to Help Balance the Throat Chakra

Relax and gently close your eyes.
Breathe deeply in and out and then visualise yourself
climbing a beanstalk, going high up into the blue sky.
Comfortably sit on a leaf or cloud
up and beyond the heavens.
There, you meet a wise man. Ask him whatever you'd like.
Know he is always there for any question you may have.
He will give you a gift,
something you need to unlock your potential.
Then climb down,
knowing you can always return any time to be with your wise man.
Begin a journal and write down all that you are told, given, and see.

The sixth chakra is known as the third eye and is located between our two physical eyes on the forehead.

The colour associated with this chakra is indigo.

This third-eye chakra is associated with our sense of awareness, our intuitive self, our psychic abilities, wisdom, faith, visualisation, and awareness.

The areas of the physical body that are connected to this chakra include the eyes, face, and some parts of the brain. Imbalance in the third-eye chakra can cause headaches, blurred vision, blindness, and eye strain.

If this chakra is imbalanced, now is the time to see the bigger picture for your life, to learn to trust your own intuition and wisdom, and to have the courage to act on your instincts. Colour has an amazing impact on balancing the chakras. To help balance this chakra, wear the colours indigo or violet.

Affirmation

"I now trust and act upon my intuition and inner vision."

A Visualisation Meditation to Help Balance the Third Eye Chakra

Relax and gently close your eyes.
Breathe deeply in and out and then visualise yourself
standing by a beautiful lake.
Peace and silence surround you.
Be still and listen.
What do you hear?
As you step into the water, you are gently pulled into a whirlpool.
Enjoy the moment as you are taken on a magical journey.
Here, you meet your guides to help you through life.
Look out for faces, images, or animals. Know you are safe.
When you see them, ask them why they have come and what message
they have for you.
Begin a journal and write down who you see and what you are told.

The seventh chakra is known as the crown chakra and is located at the top of the head.

The colour associated with the crown chakra is purple or white.

The crown chakra is associated with self-mastery, inspiration, divine purpose, detachment and faith.

The areas of the physical body that are connected to this chakra include parts of the brain, cerebral cortex, pineal gland, pituitary gland, and the central nervous system. If there is an imbalance in this chakra, we may experience migraines and depression.

If this chakra is imbalanced, you should try the following:

- Have a spiritual connection.
- Realise that not all is lost and there is light at the end of the tunnel.
- Seek a deeper understanding and connection to the universe.
- Watch without reacting to your life and the lives of others.
- Accept that what is happening is part of the divine journey and cosmic plan for your life.
- Realise that life is a journey and accept that we are here to learn and that everything happens for a reason.
- Learn about your spirituality.
- Consider and experience your connection to the concept of God or a higher intelligence.
- Colour has an amazing impact on balancing the chakras. To help balance this chakra, wear the colours purple or white or eat foods that are these colours (e.g., plums).

Affirmation

"I now surrender and have clarity of purpose."

A Visualisation Meditation to Help Balance the Crown Chakra

Relax and gently close your eyes.
Breathe deeply in and out and then
visualise yourself stepping onto a cloud.
The cloud takes you higher and higher into the heavens
like an elevator.
Think of a question you would like to ask.
The cloud stops in front of a beautiful castle.
When you walk into the castle, you see many different rooms.
You are drawn into a room full of books,
and on one of the shelves, there is a book with your name on it.
You open the book, and there lies the answer you are seeking.
This book has all the answers about you,
and you can come here anytime to seek your answers.
When you are ready, return to the cloud and go back to Earth.
Begin a journal and write all that you see, hear and read.

The keys to help you enter the spiritual room include the following:

- Realise that you are a spiritual being that has chosen to come to earth to have a human experience.
- Know that you are a unique, amazing person with gifts and talents and make the time to connect and open this amazing package you have been given.
- Have the courage to follow your soul's purpose, for this is your true GPS in life and it will lead you to joy, happiness, and riches.
- Each day, spend time connecting to your higher self and the universal energy/God.
- Always remember to show kindness and compassion.

Jackie and Jim Lindsay shared this simple yet profound tool, which allows you to constantly be in, understand, and experience the blessings and wonder of the spiritual room: be in the Now, use the white light and remember thy will not mine.

By doing these, you will be able to enter the spiritual room and gain much guidance. You will also gain the peace and stability that is currently needed to help you get through these turbulent times and give meaning to what is happening in your life.

What will you change today, to make tomorrow better?

CHAPTER 7

The Keys to the Rooms

Now that you have the keys to each room and you have entered and explored every room, let's recap briefly on the keys needed for creating a rich, healthy, happy life that you love.

The key to room 1, the physical room: Look after your health. This supports the vehicle for you to explore and enjoy life and all of its abundance.

The key to room 2, the emotional room: Emotions should be fleeting and evolving. Don't hold onto the negative ones.

The key to room 3, the mental room: Your thoughts create your reality, so think and dream positively and see the miracles happen.

The key to room 4, the spiritual room: Begin to unlock, see, and use your gifts and talents. Follow your soul's purpose because it is your GPS system and the true compass in life, the one that leads to happiness, wealth, and fulfilment. Ask for help and guidance.

CHAPTER 8

Using the Keys

If you do what you've always done,
you'll get what you've always gotten
—Anonymous

Hopefully, by now, you will have a greater awareness and understanding of the four rooms and the importance of entering them daily, even if you can only enter them for a short time because that's how you create a life you love on a sustainable basis. Entering each room daily is something that can be incorporated into your normal day if you put a little thought behind each room. Here are some ideas that can aid this process:

- We all eat and drink daily. It's a choice to incorporate regular healthy meals, wholesome snacks, and water.
- Meditation, prayer, and visualisation can all be done in bed before you even begin your day, or you can also practise before you go to sleep as well.
- We all need to get around during the day, and how we do that is a choice. Try to incorporate more walking or climb the stairs instead of taking the lift if you don't have the time to fit in an exercise program.

Life and creating a life we love is about choices—the small choices that we make every each and every day. Choose to start implementing the tips and keys discussed. By doing these little things, you begin to see big results, making you feel empowered and encouraged to keep doing them, but you have to start and do at least one thing for each room daily. Remember that each room is linked to the others, so if you neglect one room or spend too much time in another, it will affect the other rooms. In order to live and create a life you love, you must be able and willing to enter these rooms daily. Your choice!

CHECKLIST FOR CREATING A LIFE YOU LOVE

Creating a life you love is an ongoing process, but by answering yes to all of the questions below, you are on the fast track to creating a life you love. Identify any no's on your list and make an effort to focus your time and energy on these rooms so that you can balance your life and create a life that you do indeed love. By using the previous keys mentioned for entering each room on a daily basis, you gain the ability to create a life you love and experience health, wealth, and happiness.

The physical room

☐ Do you drink two litres of water daily and minimize or avoid fizzy, soft drinks and alcohol?
☐ Do you regularly eat small nutritional meals and fruit, avoiding junk/processed foods?
☐ Do you walk/exercise at least thirty minutes per day five times a week?

The emotional room

☐ Do you practise forgiveness of yourself and others?
☐ Can you control your emotions and go with the flow of life?
☐ Do you show compassion?

The mental room

☐ Are you aware that you are in control and can create the life you want?
☐ Do you use your thoughts positively to visualise a positive life for yourself?
☐ Do you know the life that you would love?

The spiritual room

☐ Do you spend time giving thanks each day for what you have in prayer or in a gratitude journal?

☐ Are you aware of your soul purpose?

☐ Do you spend thirty minutes a day in silence and alone to either meditate or commune with nature and to listen to the inner guidance of your soul?

Creating a life of health, wealth, and happiness is a journey. The destination is set by your mind, so choose to set sail for somewhere amazing. The vehicle you choose in order to travel on this journey is your body. Is your vehicle full of fuel and ready to go, or is it full of rust and running off of a flat battery? The road is your emotions; the ride can either be smooth or bumpy. The map and compass are your soul's purpose. Choose to follow it and not go blindly forward.

There will be detours on your journey. As Vivian Greene reminds us, "Life isn't about waiting for the storm to pass. It's about learning to dance in the rain." This quote means life will always through things at us. This makes us the people we are; however, by entering the rooms each day, you will be able to cope and make the most out of these detours and be able to dance in the rain.

It's never too late to blossom into the magnificent person you are and create a life you love, for the best place to start is exactly where you are now.

Bon voyage!

With love
Kerry

Special Thanks

Many people have been part of my journey. There are too many to mention individually, but thank you to all of you, especially my son, family, friends and clients.

I would like to mention some people whose work I love and who have shared their knowledge freely with me and so many others.

Many thanks to Helen Johnson for sharing her chakra meditations with us. She is an amazing friend, mentor, teacher, and homeopath. Helen runs fantastic courses. Her website is www.helenjohnson.org.

Also, many thanks to two amazing people named Jackie and Jim Lindsay. Check out their work on www.gardenof-eden.com.

THE AUTHOR

Kerry Evans-Alder is a qualified homeopath, holistic counsellor and the founder of Blossom Body & Soul, with a successful practice in Perth, Australia .Kerry's passion is to educate and empower women, helping them to activate and realise their full potential. Her special interest in women's health and wellbeing; has led her to work with women and children in third world countries, as well as in London and Australia.

Kerry can be contacted at www.blossombodysoul.com.au

RECOMMENDED AUTHORS

I am an avid reader with a wide range of recommended authors. The ones I have recommended below are the authors of easy-to-read books, and their books are also easy to obtain:

- Florence Scovel Shinn
- Catherine Ponder
- Og Mandino
- Paulo Coelho
- Napoleon Hill
- Norman Vincent Peale
- Louise Hay
- Annette Noontil
- Caroline Myss
- Brian Tracey
- Susan Hayward
- A. J. Russell (*God Calling*)